EDISON DOESN'T INVENT THE CAR

STEVE EVANS was born in Adelaide in 1952, and grew up in various South Australian country towns. An auditor who is mad on motorcycling, his poetry displays a rare appreciation of life's perplexity, diversity and humour. Some years in the making, this first collection will be gladly received by his many admirers.

Edison doesn't invent the car

STEVE EVANS

FRIENDLY STREET
POETS

**Wakefield
Press**

Copyright © 1990 Steve Evans
First published 1990
Friendly Street Poets
in association with
Wakefield Press
43 Wakefield Street
Kent Town
South Australia 5067

Promotion of this title has been assisted by the South Australian
Government through the Department for the Arts.

Cover design by Belinda Postuma
Manuscript edited by Graham Rowlands

Design and layout by John Kingsmill, Tabloid Pty Ltd,
97 Sturt Street, Adelaide, 5000

Typeset in Goudy by Adelaide Phototype Bureau Pty Ltd,
163 Halifax Street, Adelaide, 5000

Printed by Federal Printing House Pty Ltd,
20 O'Brien Street, Adelaide 5000.

ISBN 1 86254 259 7

ACKNOWLEDGEMENTS

The Australian
Bike Australia
The Bulletin Literary Supplement
The Canberra Times
Compass
Fling!
Friendly Street Poetry
        Readers No. 6, 7, 9, 10, 12, 14
Going Down Swinging
The Inner Courtyard
LiNQ
Luna
Mattoid
Northern Perspective
Pivot
Poems Public
Poetry Australia
Quadrant
Scarp
Southern Review
Times On Sunday
Unsettled Areas (ABC Radio)
Words And Visions
Wordwaves (Radio 5UV)
Writers Radio (Radio 5UV)

Edison Doesn't Invent the Car

Edison Doesn't Invent the Car 3
The Hottest Night of the Year 5
Taking it with You 7
Howard Hughes' Last Testament 8
The System 9
The Failed Tax Assessor 10
The Overthrow 12
Circumlocution 13
Kidnap 14
Murder Outside a Cinema 16
Washing the Dead (A Moslem Funeral) 17
The Coroner's Song 19
Out of Wilcannia 20
Sylvia 21
The Jump 22

Changing Partners

The Invention of Fire 27
Changing Partners 28
Hunger 29
Tourists 31
Invitation 33
Still Life with Pear 35
Hooks 36
Wire-walking 37
A Hard Bastard 38

The Pink Shoes

The Pink Shoes   41
Confetti   42
Avocado   43
Banana   44
Zucchini   45
Cats   46
Rose   47
Stars   48

Newborn

Sussex Street   51
Jigsaw   52
Stillborn   54
A Preparation for the Death of My Father   55
Room 12   56
Dying   57
The Pregnancy   58
Neighbour   59
Icon   60
Country Town   61
Birth   62
Newborn   63
Two Years Old   64
The Afternoon Nap   65
Grandfather   66

Edison Doesn't Invent the Car

Edison Doesn't Invent the Car

1.
Edison sits up with a start,
fumbles for a match.
The idea of a car
is parked around the corner.
He is thinking of something else.

2.
There is the shadow
of a car
on the wall of the bank.
As he approaches
it is momentarily obscured
by cloud.

3.
There is no shadow of a car
in the alley,
only big one-shadow,
but a soft gaseous plume
almost betrays
its hiding place.
The motor hums
quiet as a pulse.

4.
Crossing the park he senses
the round fender
the polished grille
the smell of hot chrome
sun-baked enamel.
Turning,
sees only the trees
crinoline dresses and parasols
hears only the patient clip-clopping
by picket-fence
and the limousine whir
of wind in the leaves.
Cannot put a name to it.

5.
Walks through the kitchen.
No cars crouched
on the cool slate tiles.
In the study
reaches for his glasses
in the yellow circle
under the desk-lamp.
His breath extinguishes the flame
and an unusual reflection
in the nearby picture frame.
We hear the crunch
of rubber
sneaking up the gravel path.
He doesn't notice.

6.
There is the possibility
of a car.
In his sleep
he passes us
with the throttle stuck wide
and he is laughing.
He sits up with a start
but he is thinking
of something else.

The Hottest Night of the Year

At one in the morning
you give up and turn back.
Sky's packed with clouds
brutal as big bruising trucks
jammed on a freeway
going nowhere.
On Wherret Street
the wooden garage doors still open
the mechanic greasing up his overalls
already oily black
bent over the fender
of a '62 Chevrolet
humming into the engine-bay
immune to the heat
his single light-bulb
the only glow for blocks
humidity dense as treacle
even insects sitting this one out.
No cars sulking through the streets
the soft sidewalk sucks at your shoes
and you cross by the All Night Delicatessen
with its dead neon
as dark as every house
and your screen-door swings slow
behind you
but she's not home
in a town where everybody's home
and too tired to move
except a stupid mechanic on Wherret Street
and your wife who's God knows where
and who cares
you fall on the bed
staring at the open window
the curtains don't move
and earlier you had the strength to argue
but no more
and why argue with yourself

no good running through what you said
won't change now
she might be back, might not
who knows —
everything can wait.
Even when the Chevrolet passes
and it looks like the mechanic
is not alone in there
you think it could be her too
the hair's the right length
and frankly good riddance
this heat is a bitch
if only you could sleep.

Taking it with You

(Hollywood, 1983)

It wasn't spite
but seized by the season's fever
for all things Egyptian
he dictated this peculiar
condition in his will

at least his wife and mistress
were excused the traditional
entombment and slow death
suffocating alongside the master
since apart from a blood-red Ferrari
he went to his grave alone

he'd imagined an after-life
of endless winding roads
and all the whores of Heaven
their astonishing wings folded
taking turns in the leather
passenger seat

so were the tears for him
upright at the wheel
regal in his silk pyjamas
as the bulldozer moved in
or for the wire-wheeled
Italian sarcophagus
the rare Ferrari Berlinetta
in which he sat
making his last pit-stop

Howard Hughes' Last Testament

1.
Light still haunts the hallway
like an animal
prying, licking at the door's crack.
I cannot let it in,
it would see what I am.

Sneering Jesus,
I turned the bastard to the wall.
What is forty days in the desert
compared to twenty years in hotel rooms?

2.
How pure I am
stripped of gaudy attachments,
how enviable.
Money drips from me,
my priceless skin.
It's what the world lives on,
it lubricates illusions I've no use for.
I am my cult, my adoration.
The rest is sham, tinsel.

3.
In a splinter of sunlight
a woman was tying up her hair.
How can I mourn love?
I forget what it is.

4.
Somewhere beyond this zero
the wilderness shrills its bitter lies.
Let the stars and wind dispute,
the sky decant its blue.
It does not concern me.

The System

The crack in the hallway plastered over.
Old paint stripped from the doors.
New paint on the walls.
A pergola and a fern in the yard.
The quick sale.

The new house built
in a trendy hills town near the city.
We'll make a packet, he says.
Rip off some gullible bumpkin.
And he does.

You've got to beat them
at their own game,
beat the system, he farewells,
on his way to another state,
a hobby-farm with possibilities.

In two years he'll be in Darwin
soaking in the underground economy.
Then Melbourne or Sydney a while
before the grand return.
The hair shorter at each stage,
the ambitions sharper,
the clothes greyer,
beating the system.

The Failed Tax Assessor

It wasn't silly rules
or less than glittering company.
It wasn't the two or three
who forecast
if not untimely death
at least a gruesome injury.
Sooner or later one said
we all pay.
How could I disagree?

Some tender hopeful lies.
Others bite their lips
sit on their hands
and keep their anger in
as you fill in the forms
which will break them.
A virtuous soldier
you know they've brought this
on themselves.
Faintly
by degrees
you harden
and don't notice the change.

But I did.
Tried walking more slowly
between appointments
savouring a nectarine
gazing in shop windows
other ways to delay
and pretend to forget
but always arrived on time.

Then friendly enquiries
a cup of tea and their life-story
at the kitchen table
laid out as pitifully as the receipts
and bank statements.
I'll be in touch, I'd say
as if the outcome was in doubt.
But the numbers already knew
had added themselves as easily
as an absently muttered amen.

They didn't need me.
The numbers would tell anyone.
I stepped off.

The Overthrow

A street fixture.
In all weathers the same
crumpled suit scuffed sandshoes
the old paper-man
fag permanently cornered in mouth.
Hung from a tassel of smoke
the ruined face
flinging its unintelligible cry
into the city's din.

One morning a double-take.
A similar beaten coat
frayed shirt and white hair awry
but different fingers
gnarled about the bag of change
and a clear animal call
ringing above the traffic.

For a moment more important
than the fresh headlines he waves
of disappearing planes
or governments
is this
a coup on our own corner.

Circumlocution

The river moves the river on
— Christopher Logue

Running the streets before daylight
the rhythmic slap of feet
on cold pavement
lulls me past a flicker of fences
iron, brush, brick, wire
and unlit houses one by one
varied as children rowed in a school photo
and all the same
merged in grey, unwoken —
jacarandas stir their purple
in an early draught

Going out each morning
in search of something
and always coming back
wondering what it is
until never getting to the point
becomes the point of it

Kidnap

Watching through the windscreen
rain beading on the glass
the streets strangely lit
the tiniest sound amplified
senses cramming every morsel in
and fast
so fast you feel you're accelerating
through a dream
of the rest of your life
the little left
searching for clues
and waiting for him to do something
this is your town
but never like this
sharper, more intense
it says
things have changed
this is how it really was
underneath, all the time
clear and hard
you wonder how
you could have failed to notice
still he doesn't speak
you know all the gruesome endings
all of them
but if anyone sees you passing
they'll think you husband and wife
normal
send a message!
look kidnapped!
jump out!
yes
next red light
and run like hell
but he'll follow
and then?
something jammed in the seat

cold metal under your hand
hold it, squeeze it tight
try to think
the car slows
your heart bashes crazily
this is it
at last he turns
asks if this is where
you wanted to get off
but you won't be fooled
not now
when he leans across
it will be a trick
he'll only pretend to open your door
and here it comes
he's moving
you pull your hand from the seat
and the screwdriver with it
push the thin greasy blade in
and again
this one's going to pay and pay
like the others.

Murder Outside a Cinema

Just as in the movies
he stepped out
towards his limousine
the night was perfect
a crackling luminous sky
bending neon back and forth
along the damp street
the sudden gun
black and keen as a cash-register
nudged his waistcoat
his arteries purred
already tasting the sweet rhythm
of sleep's release
the burrowing bullet announced

He handed his cigar to the assassin
casually inserted a finger
in the unpluggable wound
and would have stood there
smiling at his puzzled attacker all night
but his knees brought him down
folding neatly as a camper-chair
in one smooth movement
that closed with
the flat smack of his staring face
on the pavement

Washing the Dead

(A Moslem Funeral)

After the death of the child of a friend
who married a Moslem.

1.

Her seized baby-blue lips
refusing you,
unresponding
when you pumped your frantic air
into her coolness,
as if after six months
breathing could not be bothered
with such insignificance
and simply withdrew.
Then panic unstopped you.
Cot-death.

2.

The stupidly festive coloured glass,
its inextinguishable counterfeit warmth
lighting the slow drift of dust.
The mummifying stillness before
the candles deliver her
small and terrible
a white parcel of starched cloth
paper-sharp, cutting.
You unfold her
wincing at the coroner's embroidery
the scrawl of stitches across unhealable skin.
Something in you tightens
as the chill bowl of water arrives
for washing a Raggedy-Anne
put together wrong.
They want you to present her to heaven
clean of you,
but it is yourself you're rinsing out.

3.
You lie empty as a begging cup.
No room for it yet,
the cold fact.

The Coroner's Song

My cool family of strangers,
each a moon-pallid puzzle
awaiting my solution.
They're all here, the pretty details.
The overdoses, stranglings,
the shark's uneager customer
(or part of him).
This one came in a suitcase.
Here's a child who was smaller
than a parent's anger.

Forget what they tell you of love.
The only romance is in
the knife's gentle arc,
stripping to essentials.
Causes, effects, equations.
There is no more.

Out of Wilcannia

Two wheels hum
through the dry north.
My old motorbike
threads its myopic beam
between the soft edges
of the road,
is pulled along by this
insubstantial string of light
like a toy.

I slow a little,
squinting to distinguish
even the possibility
of glinting eyes,
the outline of a kangaroo,
anything hunched for flight
across my path.

For a while
other headlights
bob and spark
in my mirrors
then turn away
as in the darkening east
a huge black cat of cloud
shivers in a sudden crack
of electricity.

I ride toward
this dance of lightning
for hours,
hooked to
this tangling chimera
I am reeled in
faster than fear.

Sylvia

The kitchen heats slowly.
You wait again
for the first straw light of sun
cream's sour dollop
old yellow bruise.
The drab streets begin filling
with the droning tenderness
of machines wearing faces.
Same yesterday, tomorrow.

Breathe out the flame beneath
the kettle's futile hiss.
Held in the paw of this warm crucible
love is no great thing.
It occurs,
a dark possibility
persistent as a stroked cat.

There is no absolution in the vapours
but drinking this eager gas
the nudging tomorrows drowse
and sweet sleep's breath
licks your shoulders.
It is enough.

The Jump

After a report of the death of a parachutist whose unused parachute was
found to have been in working order.

Letting go.
The metal wing dips
and rolls away
glancing off the sun
drones into the glare
invisible.

Alone.
I sleek down eyes a-slit
swimming into the future.
The earth tilts
flashing senseless morse from tiny dams
that pock the fields below
and I dance
crazy groundless soft-shoe
to be here again
wave to the clouds
tiptoe towards heaven
with the nonchalant smile
of an accustomed liar.
Stretch an arm
spread five leathered fingers
curl my hand —
I am here, distinct.

Later the steel ring,
the snaking cords' escape
whipping and hissing at the clouds
the flutter of the webbing
and blue silk rippling taut as a sail
an imitation atmosphere.
But not yet.

Floating spore flecks my arm.
A hawk calmly swerves
or I swerve, hard to tell.
A lake of wheat buckled like a picnic cloth
glows in patches — yellow, soft.
A little longer.

Drain the last reserves of sky.
Let it all tip here
filtering, pulling in to this spot.
Divers in their rapture never feel
this sheer, terrifying, comfortable silence
the perfection of stillness.
Counting the seconds.
Soon, soon,
but not yet.

Changing Partners

The Invention of Fire

Her stop approaches.
The girl in front of me stands,
shakes her red hair back,
and then it happens.
As the bus leaves the shaded avenue
the light pours in
and her hair ignites.
I gape like a tourist,
want to drift my hands
through this flood of flame.
Such a fiery distraction
I forget the introduction
I've rehearsed for blocks
and abandoning care
stare too obviously
as she descends,
a torch in the suburbs.

Changing Partners

Suddenly
a maze of new objects
clutters the house
like unexpected guests
snuggling in
for a long stay.
The clothes
that shoulder yours aside
in the wardrobe,
books that displace
half your own.

You ask yourself whether
you really expected him
to step naked
from his old life
shedding attachments entirely
or merely the right ones,
those wrong ones.

Soon you'll be checking
if the toothpaste
has been changed,
or worse,
squeezed in the middle.
Then you'll count the other
previously unexposed habits
since come from hiding
and give him a list,
telling him
to pass it to his next lover.
After all,
what's the point of spite
if you can't use it well?

Hunger

We slake our thirst
mouth to mouth.
The want's bone-deep
and can't be shaken.
My hands too few,
kids in a sweet-shop
loitering at one delight
while giddily craving the next.
The amazing convexities
the offerings of arc
and circle.
You turn to let a breast
weigh itself in my hand.

We nip and bruise in play
give up to dazzle and
disarray,
sheets and pillows strewn
the bed can hardly contain
us.
You pull me down
and fall back laughing.
We're skin-slipping
and kiss-sticky.
The heat's in us.

We stroke and sigh
on the edge of trance,
a slow languorous sinking
soft as the afternoon shadows
that laze into the room
dappling us like
fish in a sleepy pond.
Your hair's alight in my fingers,
the day's last flaring.
I dip my tongue in the hollow
your collarbone makes,
shape a necklace of kisses.
It is loving work.

The dark laps in,
its gradual erasure
of door, chair, clothes
making us an island
of touch and warmth.
Your breathing slows
and soon you ride a long dream.
I watch the line
of your body
faint against the window.
Its rise and fall is my pulse
my measure,
and you my welcome addiction.

My opium
my love
with you
always
the hunger.

Tourists

Beside her pale body
you lie watching day break,
and wonder.
When you arrived
the air was unnaturally clear,
a brilliance and depth
so beguiling
you dismissed the suspicion
of some dark thing
hidden from view.
Strange country.

More coups than South America
but a government invisible.
Borders in constant flux
but no foreign policy
to speak of.
The flag seems to change
with the washing
and there are as many
national anthems
as favourite songs.
Strange country.

Only tourists live here.
The map shows a hinterland
of curfew and exile
that explains the inward rush,
a willingness to mortgage all.
You danced the streets with them,
laughing under coloured lights
where even debt-collectors
wore party hats
and seemed to smile.
Strange country.

One morning you'll wake
and find it gone —
a bare field
where the carnival's been.
Strange country,
love.

Invitation

The meeting and
the awkward parting
of lips
or hearts
is old ceremony.
In doorways
on river-banks
in kitchens after midnight
and long conversation.
The lovers' shrines.
Come to them with hope
or without.
Come expecting anything,
maybe fearing it also.

Here the clumsy
are beautiful in betrayal,
surprised at how easily
it is done to them
by them.
Tears in the driver's seat
when the key won't stay
still enough to fit.
And for each of these
another whose hunger's
beyond translation
who's felt the white heat
and wants that jolt again
a firewalker
who'll not be burnt
if only faith enough.

I want to take you now
take you to the river
and a search-light moon.
The clouds are cat's-cradling
in a bright sky.
Leave your other lover sleeping.
Grab a coat only.
You needn't believe
a thing you'll say,
as long as I can
see you.

Still Life with Pear

A slowing,
the sky empties
as if the earth inhaled
dragging all birds
down to solid things.
Wind stills.
A shadow pauses in your garden.
The cat crouching under the camellias
disowns my gaze.
You slap the sheet softly
to claim me from the window.
I turn to join you on the bed.

The flimsy compliments my lips confer
mean as little as the gauze of sunlight
caught in the terse spikes
of your short blonde hair,
due recognition only.
My mouth attends your thigh.
You reach for a pear
on the bedside table.
"Loving you
is like living on a faultline,"
I offer,
watching your first bite
open the dripping fruit.

Wiping juice from your chin
you toss the core away,
brush sticky fingers across my shoulder.
"Love is a fiction," you laugh.
We begin.

Hooks

Keeping the light on a little longer
for waiting
for just in case.
Each car down the street
sounds at first like his,
lifts your head from the book.
You read a page twice, three times,
mechanically,
finally put aside that pretence.

Rain pummels the window.
You turn off the light
swearing to think only of sleep
but can't stop these useless
soundings in familiar waters.
His hunger fills you,
a cruel, occasional feast
that merely whets your appetite.

In this room
one breath burns in reply
to an unarriving question.
There will be more cars growling by,
hours before darkness diminishes him.

Wire-walking

Light from your window
spills into the overgrown driveway
like a bright gusting cloth.
In the dark street
the car's cooling engine ticks
off the reasons to leave.
I refuse to listen,
duck the clawing tangle of roses
to your door.
You answer quickly.

In the lounge-room
the conversation cautiously genuflects
to children and marriages
that clutter the space between us
like mines in a shipping lane.
During the obligatory coffee
a careful path is steered
to the first accidental touch.
The rest is an easy slide.

A Hard Bastard

You find yourself thinking
ungraciously
that someone should be filming this,
she does it so well.
Blue light pours from her eyes
a sad pulse of questions
that changes nothing.
Your affection's a meagre annuity
wheeled out for anniversaries
or the purchase of a bargain.
You're a hard bastard, you know
but it's only survival
knowing when to cut and run.
She dabs her eyes.
Outside the car
the pines sift the fog
a skirt of mist
hugging their damp trunks.
She's stopped talking
at last.
Maybe soon it will be over.

The Pink Shoes

The Pink Shoes

They take nothing seriously.
Slip-on cartoons of shoes
that curve about her ankles.
They skid and lark like kids
outside a circle of parents,
clowning on the periphery
of your solemn conversations.
Lolling street-corner subversives
taking the mickey.
Tongue-less tongue-pokers.

They can always stare you down.
Incredulous gaping pink mouths
of perpetual mock astonishment.
Shocking pink pranksters
flagrant as flamingoes.
Pink as passion.
Unsubdued.
Unpedestrian.
Only secondarily
shoes.

Confetti

1.
basic as atoms
they are social creatures
tiny explorers
which sneak inside collars
and hide in bras

specially adapted to
live in your hair and underwear
some strains survive for years
but most like papery plankton
soon disappear

2.
they're a peppering of coloured holes
two-dimensional spotlights
for microscopic performers

they like to imitate strewn petals
a shower of almond blossoms
carelessly punctuating
fullstops that freckle the pavement
a path of icing pink and wedding white

3.
their peculiar family tree includes
raindrops
100s and 1000s and paint spots
and more distantly
city lights and Morse dots

4.
persistent party-goers
and prodigious multipliers
their future's assured
it's a short half-life
but a merry one

Avocado

a geometer's fancy
this bell of frog-skin
with its parabolas
cupping a circle of stone
a green scrotum
for one perfect ball

a missed link
or a rebound from
one of evolution's dead-ends
a reptilian hide
confused by trees
and other culinary possibilities
which might otherwise have been
the first amphibious fruit

Banana

I lift it up and pinch
one dark-nippled end
the smooth skin
a wet-suit of safety-yellow
splits crisp and fibrous

in the bowl it had been
a dash among dots
crossing the round reds
and circular greens
no chance of camouflage
its only defence this curious
pointing in two directions at once
advertising an apple's shine
and there the succulent
promise of a pear
but who could ignore
this tropical crescent moon?

the exposed flesh is fluted
and etched with a delicate
unreadable cuneiform
a message
in the strangest bottle

Zucchini

As exotically named
as a rare foreign sports car
or an acrobatic circus troupe
but as common as Smiths
a surfeit of light-haired
unknuckled fingers
permanently grounded little zeppelins
multiplying as furiously
as a B-grade movie's
sci-fi invasion force

sliced for salads
or sauteed in butter
and lemon juice
or one of 63 other ways
but not enough
one plant's an embarrassment of riches
as useless as Confederate dollars
the original overachievers
and the inspiration
for Z.P.G.

Cats

From the verandah
I watch them come and go
sauntering like indolent gods
to private feline melodies.
Their yellow silences swallow me
as they pass.
Pink-mouthed sun-seekers
leoparding in the vine overhead,
professional hedonists
the original leisured-class,
idle bags of sleep, contentment,
that stir in an arching concord of muscle
then settle again
tongue-rasping, proprietary-eyed.

These innocents
the banshees of last night,
the tuneless buskers at my window?
Someone else, they suggest,
lapsing into Egyptian postures
of omniscience.

Rose

In a slim glass
by the window
a solitary red rose
inclines slightly
watching its reflection

Uncomplicated by cloud
the night-sky turns
will disclose in an hour
the brilliant moon

Then in this room
a cool bathing radiance
and at its heart
a single red
crystal of fire

Stars

Lying flat on the earth
and staring straight up
you see them
at first like dust-specks
on a negative
these unsolicited
messages from strangers
heavenly junk-mail
vast histories
compressed into these spots
before the eyes
an indiscriminate interstellar gossip
beyond language
and out of date

each sky an album
of every other
and you think you begin to grasp it
the part containing the whole
for a moment it teases
almost there
the one pulse
energy
the One
but it wriggles away
leaves only a sheet of sparks
ascending from the oldest grinding wheel

Newborn

Sussex Street

My grandfather
a photograph only,
a small man in a cardigan
by a rosebush,
black and white.
I'm told of proud walks to the pub
with a son towering on either side
but he is alone here
in his braces and baggy trousers,
squinting at the lens.

And his father
sepia and stiff-backed
on the mantlepiece also.
Full moustache and officer's cap
brooding over the seated family
faces impassive for posterity,
straw-hats and ribbons
cane chairs on the lawn
by a cool stone verandah.
1914 formal.

In this jacaranda street
two men I never knew,
one digging his garden
and the other solemn military face
forever locked in the Victorian shadow,
paternal, strict
admitting no fear.

There must be more.

Jigsaw

1.

A sulphurous shock of cockatoos
announces dusk
shivers from the trees
at the head of the valley
and flickers past
spilling down towards the dam.
The evening breeze follows
scuffing low and tossing my hair.
Last in train
my sister's almost musical devotions
at the piano
seep from the house and gust away.
I close my eyes and am lifted.

2.

High in two broad hands
a speechless child turned like a gem
in the light for inspection.
My father lowers me
to cotton sheets damp with fever
as dewed grass
and I roll in a downhill blur
of limbs' crazy semaphore
into childhood.
At the bottom my hands
spotted, wrinkled leather
older than I ever was
among the green.

3.
I clutch to my mother's skirt.
I crouch at her grave.
Hold and let go.
The murmur of white coats,
of birthday candles.
I climb trees into dizzying blue.
Fragments of youth, old age
disordered as a dropped jigsaw
that nothing can pull together.
A shadow at the window.
In a distant part of the building
someone tinkers at a piano
starts it all over.
It's supposed to be quiet where we lie.

Stillborn

At first
you scrawled noiselessly,
a mute, sulking
reclusive shadow of ourselves
invisibly spidering,
weaving us together.

But you stilled,
went limply bobbing in the fog,
a foetal Mary Celeste
drifting like the ghost
of nothing that ever lived.
Had we let our faith waver?
Had we too much?
The absurd guilts revolve.

Indifferently,
they laid you a few hours
in a room by the nursery,
cold as moon's clean washing light,
unmoved by this world.
Next to those garrulous dolls
you preached unenviable solitude,
casual as gravity.

A Preparation for the Death of My Father

In the drizzling garden you unstoop
head shrouded in clouds of breath
and peer into the emphysemic sky.
Age withered your horizons
shrinking them back to your own size.
With a fierce inexorable patience
the logic of decay
persuades your bleak flesh.

Fear has become your companion
dragging you about like a ghost.
You huddle against its invisibility
hoping to be overlooked.
So pale I could walk through you.
Can I be a god,
firm a hold on this evaporating man?

I address this to an illusion.
Soon even that will dissipate —
the wet garden shimmer then clarify,
leaving only the absence of you.
I worry words into a funeral armour.
Your body fails you
as I must do.

Room 12

Moored by tubes
you hold to the world shakily.
Your handwriting more and more
like a child's
though the simple bony sentences
still grip facts tight as molecules.
Your children are blank spectators
briefly tendering lips
to this wrinkled kissing wraith.
Even your interest is waning,
despite the flowers
left like a trophy
a great futile optimism
beside your bed.

Dying

On the steel bedside-cabinet
the string of cards,
all the bright-eyed widows
writing to regret.
The inky topography of the medical chart
jagged as glass
the only peaks in a cool wasteland.
Nurses like small
wind-stalled yachts
on a pure horizon.
The needles
little electrical jolts
receding,
happening elsewhere,
miniature percussions of a distant war.

Old age.
It is some other body failing
bleaching in the crisp white silences,
like the photos
in albums of the gone dears.

The Pregnancy

When you exercise
the cats satellite
in milling orbit
drinking energy
the house is filling
with brazen fragrances
the atmosphere redolent
with the sweet announcements
of lotions and powders
discarded towels lie
like lazing animals
they fall
from your wet black hair
or rounded belly
to lounge on chairs
and the unmade bed
like indifferent sunning
predators
in an ancient royal court

At the new cursive fluency
of your movement
the world becomes tiny
undaunting
and you are redefined
a smiling continent adrift
assuming the strengths
of large things
your grace is terrifying
an airy sailing
through these cluttered rooms
where gravity suspends

Neighbour

His only communication
is this secretive lopping,
the wattle by our mutual fence
shorn flat where it threatened
his driveway.
Other wreckage we discover
on our waking round.
Here the split trunk
there torn branches
that signpost his anger.
It fumes and eddies silently
in his rectangle, his territory,
nervously slapping and slashing
against the length of the border
like a beast pacing its cage
not because it can't get out
but because the next creature
is trying to come in.

Icon

for Janis

In the museum display
a small line of them under glass,
the primitive pregnant gods of stone
which waited like patient divers
on the seabed of prehistory
for the tug from the surface.

When you sit, doing nothing,
you mimic their rotund benign expressions
and I understand
how awestruck cavers crouched in ash
to fashion replicas of you.
On those squat pear-shapes
gently revolving in rough hands
the cryptic smile
that sings in our stars also.

Country Town

for David, my brother

The dull seared paddocks grew me
the monosyllabic silo
the slow motion of cricket
on a dustbowl oval
the railway siding
with its mirage of patient grain-trucks
in a liquid shimmering of road

Sitting at the screen-door
watching the haze
over the flat stubbled fields
the cloudless autarchy of sky
slowly refining to heat-lightning
a small lizard cat-sunning
in the last brilliance
that streaks between the palings
the same light scything
the strip of grass by the roadside
a suspicion of southerly wind
raising temporary hope of rain
the careful diction of first drops
dust-puffing on footpaths

Now though I sometimes drive
through the glare of the same wheat-belt
I skirt the town
leave the island of childhood intact
there it remains
always 1958

Birth

for Janis and Jared

Your attendants diminish,
their conversation drifting away
like elusive short-wave voices
during childhood nights by the radio.
In the dimmed room
even your bright gasps fade.
In the still heart of pain
a clear focus of self,
of muscle, tissue and will.

Out of the sharp breaths and straining
he emerges,
first the small cap of dark hair
slick as a licked kitten,
our Valentino,
and then in a bloody rush
the lithe plunging body
sheathed in white vernix
like a greased Channel-swimmer
and smelling sweet as musk.
For a moment the cobalt eyes
regard us with an incongruous,
      unsettling calm
cool as china —
then the despairing human cry

Newborn

How could he have prepared
for this angry welcome to need?
There it was quiet as a country pond
only the frog-creak of leaning bones
and blood's commuting like a distant wind
when he flexed
in the known world of circles
practising Arm, Leg
kicking like a cat in a bag.
Was it this trembling escapee
whose confidence we mapped
this mewing, wet Houdini
helplessly fisting at the light?
Though inflated with burning air
his startled antique face
even now flickers with want
the greedy, ready mouth
singing a perfect O.

Two Years Old

You run the street to me
then refuse my hand, independent.
Already the losses begin.
Other ownerships contend,
claiming you.
The distances you take
in your tiny stride
we fret over,
won't let ourselves learn
to let go.

Of all your careful phrases
you've mastered best
the uses of No,
yet still give yourself away,
dancing in the kitchen
the day's news
in an impromptu song.

We wake sometimes
to find your body
a question mark
curled between us.

The Afternoon Nap

The house is quiet
a cool harbour in summer
the muttering fridge
the halfhearted flap of a blind
In the shaded room
the mother and child
His pursed lips in sleep
are miniatures of hers
seem on the verge of speaking
His skewed hair
arrows urgently in all directions
contradicting the limp body

The temperatures inside and out
slowly compromise
In an hour or so
the sleepers separately stir
and sensing themselves awake
rummage for the other faces I know
pulling them on like oxygen masks

Grandfather

He must have paused
a hand grey with cement
tipping back the stained hat
and looked down on the grid
of the cottage town in the copper district
the crumbling mounds of old tailings
the regular rows of iron roofs
baking like loaves
easily picking out his own
or swigged from the water-bag
and peered across the paddocks
toward the blank sea
before returning to the trowel
eighty feet up
building the silo

Evening's slow walk
corners as familiar as his callouses
a cloud of cement dust shaken off
in the frail wash-house
a long draught of rainwater
before politely knocking
at his own back door

I meet him by touching
the simple things he knew —
      violets he tended in the stony yard
      the cool enamel of the kerosene fridge
      the huge glowing dial of the shortwave
      and those black companions on a high shelf
      the heavy family Bible
      and the medical encyclopaedia
in all a strange acquaintance

Was it seeing from so high
those Little Cornwall streets
that spelt his 50 years
or out of endless churching
some mad prayer lured him
stepping into air
or was he free of such notions
when the rusty roofs went whirling
and the haze of stubbled wheat-fields
was revolving in his eye?

Grandfather
you shared this name
you knew what hands could do
tell me
why they never speak of you
what silenced them
was it the life or the leaving?

FRIENDLY STREET POETS

The Leichardt Heater Journey by Larry Buttrose
Trader Kate and The Elephants by Kate Llewellyn
Dial-A-Poem by Graham Rowlands
Death as Mr. Right by Jeri Kroll
over the outrow by Rory Harris
The Crack in the Crib by Mike Ladd
Messages of Things by K.F. Pearson
the white rose & the bath by Jenny Boult
Caught on the Hop by Rob Johnson
Leaving Maps by Jeff Guess
The Bay of Salamis and Other Poems by John Bray
No Collars No Cuffs by Geoff Goodfellow
Beware the Bougainvillea by Donna McSkimming
the bitumen rhino by Neil Paech
in the half-light by Louise Crisp & Valery Wilde
Other Ways of Looking by Constance Frazer
snapshots from a moving train by Rory Harris
On the Menu by Graham Rowlands
The Fernhouse Cure by Barry Westburg

FRIENDLY STREET POETS
&
WAKEFIELD PRESS

Edison Doesn't Invent the Car by Steve Evans
The Inner Courtyard: A South Australian Anthology of
Love Poetry edited by Anne Brewster and Jeff Guess

These titles are currently available from
Wakefield Press
Box 2266,
Kent Town
South Australia 5071
Telephone (08) 362 8800

THE FRIENDLY STREET
POETRY READERS

The Friendly Street Poetry Reader
edited by Richard Tipping (AUUP)

Number Two Friendly Street Poetry Reader
edited by Ian Reid & Andrew Taylor (AUUP)

Number Three Friendly Street Poetry Reader
edited by Larry Buttrose & Peter Goldsworthy (AUUP)

No. 4 Friendly St. Poetry Reader
edited by Span & Jenny Boult

No. 5 Friendly St. Poetry Reader
edited by Nancy Gordon & K.F. Pearson

No. 6 Friendly St. Poetry Reader
edited by Anne Brewster & Rob Johnson

No. 7 Friendly St. Poetry Reader
edited by John Bray & Jan Owen

No. 8 Friendly St. Poetry Reader
edited by Robert Clark & Jeri Kroll

No. 9 Friendly St. Poetry Reader
edited by Graham Rowlands & Pauline Wardleworth

No. 10 Friendly St. Poetry Reader
edited by Rory Harris & Beate Josephi

No. 11 Friendly St. Poetry Reader
edited by Elaine Golding & Peter McFarlane

No. 12 Friendly St. Poetry Reader
edited by Jeff Guess & Donna McSkimming

No. 13 Friendly St. Poetry Reader
edited by Constance Frazer & Barry Westburg

No. 14 Friendly St. Poetry Reader
edited by Ann Timoney Jenkin and Neil Paech

These titles are currently available from
Wakefield Press
Box 2266, Kent Town
South Australia 5071
Telephone (08) 362 8800

Friendly Street Poetry readings are held
at the Box Factory, Regent Street, Adelaide
on the first Tuesday night of every month
(except January).

WAKEFIELD PRESS
LITERARY TITLES

Arcadian Adelaide, Thistle Anderson
Bleak Rooms, Peter Goldsworthy
Bow Tie & Tails, Geoff Goodfellow
Clara Morison, Catherine Helen Spence
Double Destiny, ed. K.F. Pearson
Mapped But Not Known, ed. P.R. Eaden & T.F. Mares
Mars in Scorpio, Kurt von Trojan
No Collars No Cuffs, Geoff Goodfellow
Not Only in Stone, Phyllis Somerville
Painting the Town, Jeff Guess
Patrick White Speaks, Patrick White
Rites of Arrival, Jeff Guess
Satura, John Bray
Seventy-seven, John Bray
The Orange Tree, ed. K.F. Pearson & Christine Churches
Under the Pepper Trees, ed. Marcie Muir
Unsettled Areas, ed. Andrew Taylor
Walking to Bethongabel, Robert Clark
Zooing, Peter Goldsworthy

These titles are currently available from

Wakefield Press
Box 2266
Kent Town
South Australia 5071
Telephone (08) 362 8800